IMAGES
of America

AROUND
HERNDON

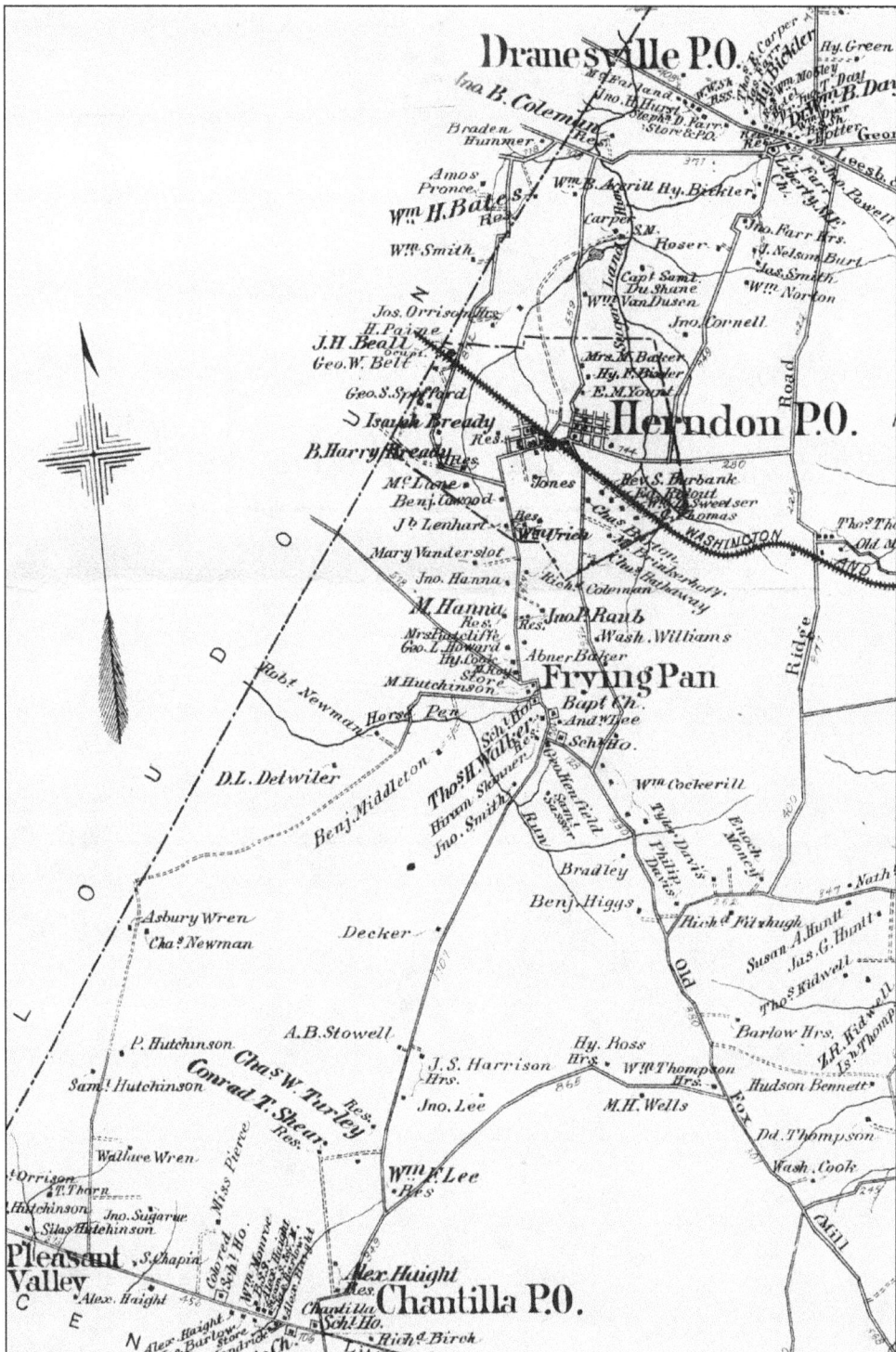

This map is reproduced from G. M. Hopkins's *Atlas of Fifteen Miles Around Washington, D.C.*, 1878. (Courtesy Wm. Edmund Barrett and the Pioneer America Society, Inc., by the Friends of the Fairfax County Public Libraries.)

IMAGES
of America

AROUND
HERNDON

Margaret C. Peck

ARCADIA
PUBLISHING

This is a seal created for the town of Herndon by Anthony DeBenedittis. It was adopted by the town council on June 8, 1976.

CONTENTS

ACKNOWLEDGMENTS

The author would like to thank the Herndon Historical Society, the Fairfax County Library, and Alice M. Burton for use of prints from their collections. In addition, thanks go to members of area families who so graciously loaned photographs from their family albums and to Mary H. Lowe and D. Porter Hutchison for their support of this project.

INTRODUCTION

Even today if you walked across a ploughed field after a rain in the area around Herndon, including the communities of Floris, Chantilly, Pleasant Valley, and Dranesville, you would have a chance of finding arrowheads. Or if you searched along Cain's Branch at Chantilly, Horsepen Run at Floris, or Cub Run at Pleasant Valley you might find some there. When the soil was moved for the building of Dulles International Airport, workers found hundreds of arrowheads, enough to fill many buckets.

Before the middle 1700s, landowners from the Tidewater area of Virginia were obtaining grants for land in this northern section, and after receiving a grant they in turn leased smaller sections to others. Among the individuals having grants for large tracts here were Fitzhugh, Carter, Barnes, Awbrey, Lee, Turberville, Tayloe, and Berkley. Herndon is built on land held by Carter and Barnes.

Farming became a way of life for many, but a number became tradesman to take care of the needs of others. A shoemaker, a blacksmith, and a carpenter were among the first to offer services. Maps were made to mark and name places while Indian paths were improved to become roads. One of the earliest roads was Ox Road, called West Ox Road in this northwestern section. Route 7 north of Herndon was an early road used by drovers taking animals and other goods to market. Route 50—Little River Turnpike—was another.

By the last quarter of 1700, homes that had been constructed as cabins were added to in order to have a fine house, or a completely new home was constructed. George Payne, the nephew of a friend of George Washington, had built a house in today's Herndon by 1783, Richard Bland Lee directed the building of a home in Chantilly in 1794, and John Coleman built Elden in Herndon in 1794. Andrew Hutchison had a brick home at Pleasant Valley by 1790, and George Richard Lee Turberville had Leeton at Chantilly by 1794. When John Davis, around 1800, walked to Newgate (Centreville) he found four log huts and a Meeting House at Frying Pan. Only the Meeting House is still in place.

What became Herndon was considered a village, as were the smaller clusters of homes around it. Dranesville, named after Washington Dran, had the first church, first tavern, and first post office; however, they lost out to grow as a town when the railroad took the path through Herndon.

By the middle 1800s, newcomers were making an appearance. Quakers came from New York and Pennsylvania, and others came from the South. Along with growth and change, there was the realization that a post office was needed for Herndon. The citizens worked together to come up with a name for their town, and after several attempts someone suggested the name Herndon. Capt. William Lewis Herndon had recently been lost at sea when his ship went down off Cape Hatteras. The post office in Herndon opened on July 13, 1858. Chantilly had had a post office since 1830, Frying Pan by 1889, and Pleasant Valley in the early 1900s.

Herndon and its surrounding communities were affected by the Civil War, but no major battle was fought here. Dranesville had one battle and six skirmishes. John S. Mosby and his Rangers were often in the Frying Pan section, and Laura Ratcliff, Mosby's local contact, lived on Centreville Road. Mosby made a raid on Herndon in March 1863, and the Meeting House served as a layover site and a place for the injured.

By 1878, Herndon had two steam mills, three churches, five stores, a wheelwright, and several smaller places of business. Dranesville, Frying Pan, and Chantilly each had mills, too. The railroad had been completed to Herndon by 1857 and to Leesburg by 1860. On January 14, 1879, the Commonwealth of Virginia approved a charter for Herndon, making it the second incorporated town in Fairfax County. At one time, with its progress and growth, Herndon was considered the business hub of the county, and also contained the largest building.

The 1900s found the town of Herndon and the outlying villages busy with dairy farms and businesses and workers riding the train to Washington to work, shop, and play. Dairy farmers shipped milk to Washington by train and truck, and in 1920 the Milk Producers Association was established. This section became known for its outstanding dairy farms, and animals raised here were sought by others. On the farms, record field crops were grown for feed and sale as new methods were used.

Community organizations were forming—the Farmers Club, Fortnightly Club, Grange, and others. During this time people in the city found the country a fine location for summer days. They could take the train to Herndon or Loudoun County, where there were boarding houses to accommodate them. It wasn't long before the new visitors requested the names Snickersville and Frying Pan be changed to Bluemont and Floris.

The Depression years had an effect, but life continued, and people learned to cope. Many are the memories families have of church, school, and community activities—ice cream festivals, school programs, family visiting, and farmers helping each other at harvest. Not to be forgotten were the wonderful meals served by the host family. World Wars I and II were times when the town and villages worked together for our country. A shipment of flour for France became a day of celebration with music and speeches. A drive for scrap iron, rationing, or working the spotter station were all taken on. Victory when it came was sweet, but hearts remembered with sadness those who did not return from either war.

Education was seen as extremely important, and the early schools were enlarged and improved. Students from the outlying areas were attending high school in Herndon by 1930. Travel improved when the road from Herndon to Floris was hard-surfaced in 1903 and on beyond by 1925. The homemaker's days eased with the addition of electric equipment—a stove in the kitchen, a vacuum cleaner, and a sewing machine.

By 1958, 10,000 acres of land had been marked for a new airport, and by 1962, Dulles International Airport had been constructed and dedicated. All of this brought additional people, houses, automobiles, and commercial establishments. As a result, Herndon today has a population of 22,500-plus and still growing. It is one of four towns in a county with a population of one million. Herndon and the local villages have grown, but they continue to work together in positive ways.

One

SCENES AROUND HERNDON

Isaiah Bready, who served as the first mayor for the town of Herndon, built this stone home in 1876. Today Bready's great-grandson George Price and his wife, Laura, live in the home and are active participants in Herndon activities.

This panorama may have been photographed from the west side of town in the area of the

This aerial view shows a portion of Station Street. The photograph was probably taken from the roof of a building at the intersection of Pine and Monroe Streets. (Courtesy Herndon Historical Society, J. Berkley Green Collection.)

Bready farm. (Courtesy Alice M. Burton.)

Holden Harrison took this aerial photograph from the top of the water tower at Vine and Center Streets. St. Timothy's Episcopal Church is at the corner of Elden and Grace Streets on the right. Far into the back center, the school can be seen. Most of the houses on Elden Street are still in place. (Courtesy Herndon Historical Society, J. Berkley Green Collection.)

The train tracks were placed in an area that gave the depot a prime spot in what became the town center. Both business and social activities took place in this area during earlier years and continue to do so today. (Courtesy Alice M. Burton.)

With this photograph you are looking to the east with the depot on the right. The large barn west of the depot was lost in the early 1930s due to an electrical storm. If you look beyond the depot the Reed home, or "Yellow House," can be seen. This building was later moved to the left and the present funeral home placed in that location. For a period of time school was held in this house. (Courtesy Herndon Historical Society, J. Berkley Green Collection.)

Farmers from the town and around Herndon stand on the platform and wait for the train to arrive. The cans of milk were brought to the station and the empty cans were picked up when that day's milk was put on the train. Passengers wait in front of the station for the train. (Courtesy Alice M. Burton.)

This is a photograph of the building that served as a hardware store for many years. The Schneiders ran a business from 1909 until 1919, and then from 1919 until 1968 the Duddings had the store. Charlie Reed of Herndon was the builder. Today this space is a parking lot. (Courtesy Alice M. Burton.)

This is the Walker Building, which was located at the corner of Pine and Station Streets. Some individuals were concerned that this large, three-story building might topple, until they better understood the manner of construction. (Courtesy Herndon Historical Society, J. Berkley Green Collection.)

Shoppers mingle in front of the Walker Building. This building at one time had the distinction of being the largest building in Fairfax County. (Courtesy Alice M. Burton.)

This postcard shows the Sweetser House with a small building adjacent to it. This addition was used as a post office when Republicans held office. When Democrats held office the post office was located on the south side of town. Mr. Sweetser served as postmaster. (Courtesy Alice M. Burton.)

LOCAL AND LONG DISTANCE TELEPHONE CONNECTIONS

W. H. TAYLOR, REAL ESTATE AGENT,

HERNDON, VIRGINIA

OFFICE IN THE

Trains Lv
Washingt'n
for Herndon
A. M.
8:10
P. M.
1:30, 4:20,
5:05, 6:25

—

Herndon for
Washingt'n
A. M.
5:40, 7:02
8:13
P. M.
1:3 , 6:34

NORTHERN VIRGINIA

FARMS

AND

VILLAGE HOMES

FOR SALE

AND

EXCHANGE.

SEND FOR PRICE LIST
AND MAP.

TAYLOR HOUSE

LOCATED NEAR DEPOT AND POSTOFFICE

Here is a postcard used as an advertisement by W.H. Taylor, a real estate agent in Herndon. His advertisement also gives information regarding the train schedule to and from Washington, D.C. (Courtesy Alice M. Burton.)

15

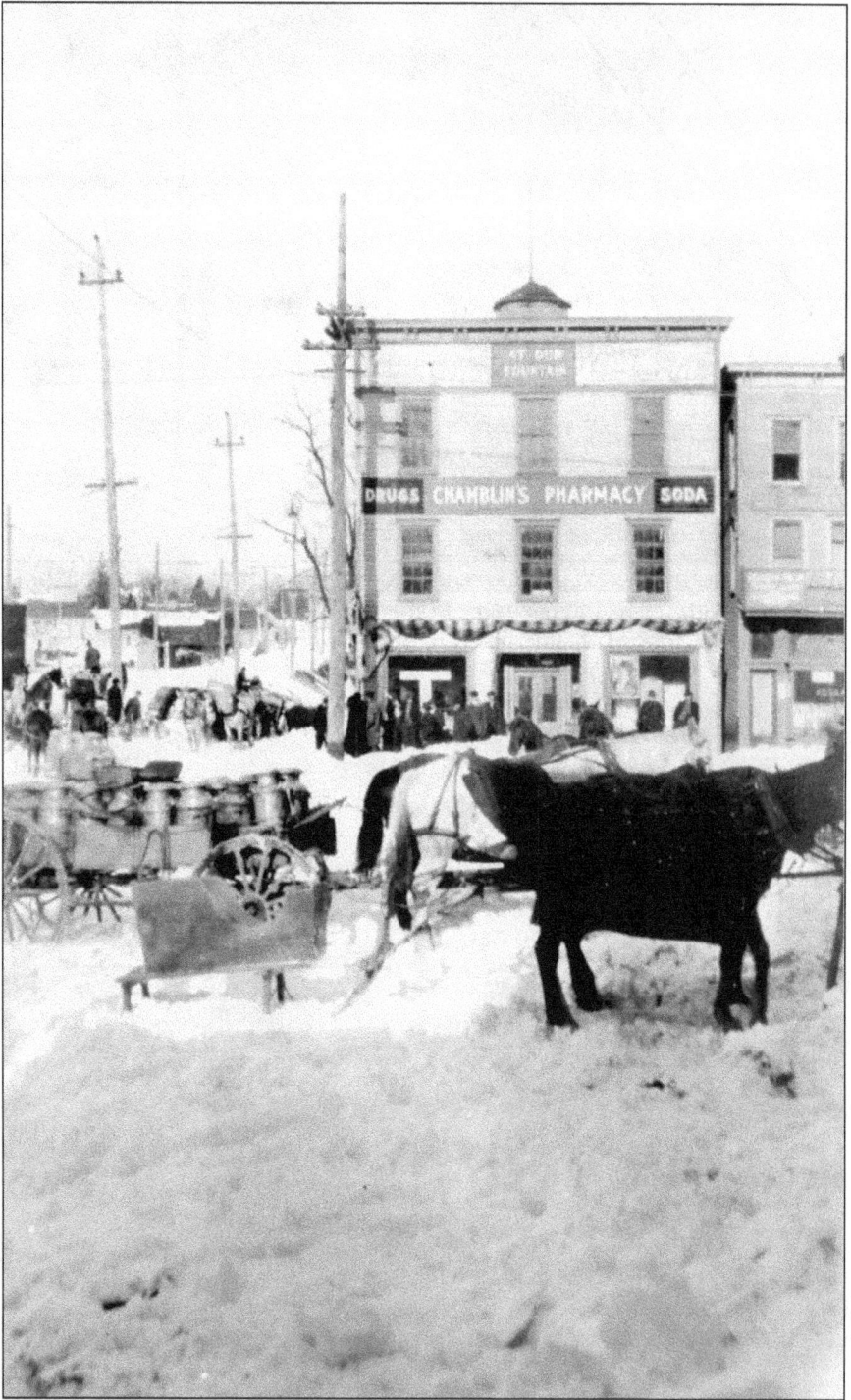

Pictured on this postcard is the day after a heavy snowfall in 1922. Empty milk cans had been picked up from the station and the filled cans of milk have been put on the train. Farmers and others are visiting in front of Chamblin's Pharmacy while horses, wagons, and sled wait. (Courtesy Alice M. Burton.)

The brick building seen in this photograph was on the east side of the depot. It was called the Dymo Building and was used to provide electricity for the trains. The people in the buggy could be waiting for passengers to leave the train. (Courtesy Herndon Historical Society, J. Berkley Green Collection.)

This is a photograph of the Herndon Packing House, which was located at Center and Vine Streets. Humme and Robinson's Milling Company and International Harvester were at this location later. They were followed by several other business ventures. (Courtesy Herndon Historical Society, J. Berkley Green Collection.)

The photograph shown on this postcard was taken near the intersection of Elden and Monroe Streets, looking west. The large building on the right was a mill. (Courtesy Alice M. Burton.)

The National Bank of Herndon was started in 1935 with funds from the community. In the early 1960s, a wing was added on the north side of the building. Today, it is home to Community Bank of Northern Virginia and the Great Harvest Bread Company uses the addition. (Courtesy Herndon Historical Society, J. Berkley Green Collection.)

An employee of Mr. Asbury Harrison is watching after the Harrisons' mule team. They are waiting in front of the Schneider/Dudding Hardware Store. At the present time, there is no building on this lot. (Courtesy Herndon Historical Society, J. Berkley Green Collection.)

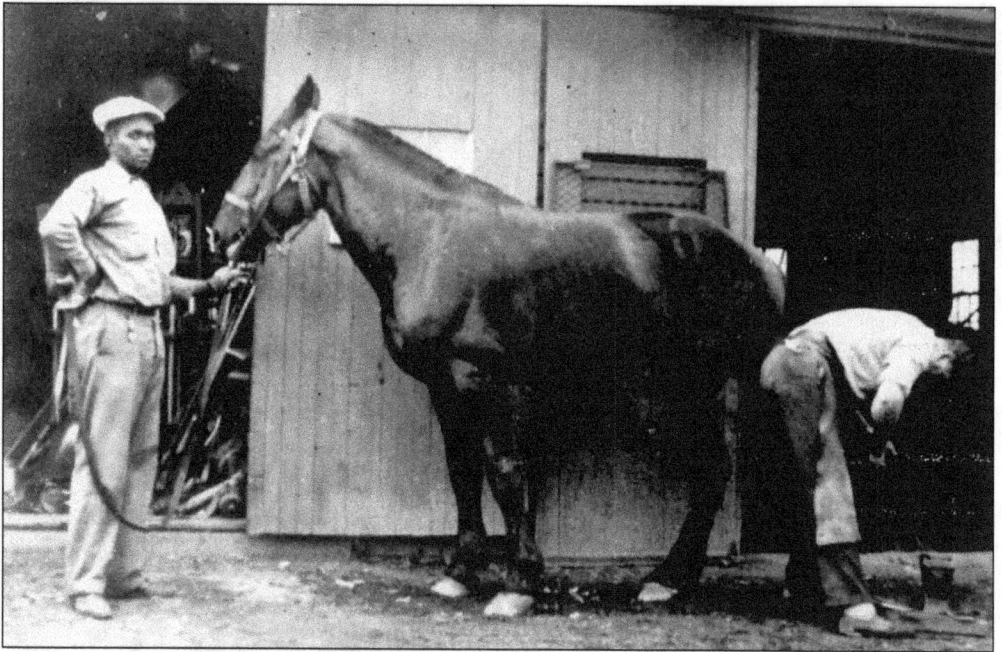

Henry Moffett opened his blacksmith shop in 1918 and closed it in 1970. He was the fifth generation of his family to care for the needs of farmers and other community individuals. Mr. Moffett shoed horses and worked on farm equipment. Today the blacksmith shop is located at Frying Pan Park. (Courtesy Herndon Historical Society, J. Berkley Green Collection.)

Five Herndon gentlemen appear ready for a train ride, while the porter stands to the right of the train. The men are, from left to right, E.E. Gillette, K. Utterback, a Washington and Old Dominion (W&OD) Railroad official, Arthur Buell, and Dr. Ernest Robey. (Courtesy Herndon Historical Society, J. Berkley Green Collection.)

In this postcard photograph, the snow has been pushed aside and carriages make their way to the station. (Courtesy Alice M. Burton.)

Shown here is a tree being taken down in front of the Crippen Furniture Store on Station Street. The telephone office and the library were located on the second floor of the building. During the fire of 1917, this building was lost. (Courtesy Alice M. Burton.)

This view of the town center is from the north side of the depot. The businesses are, from left to right, Duddings Hardware, the News Shop, Nachmans, and the Herndon Hotel. The hotel later served as business/office space. The automobiles are c. 1916 Fords. (Courtesy Herndon Historical Society, J. Berkley Green Collection.)

John Walter White (left) and Herbert Coates (right) appear to be deep in conversation while observing the aftermath of the 1917 fire. (Courtesy Herndon Historical Society, J. Berkley Green Collection.)

Mrs. W.W. Taylor is shown using a temporary telephone on Station Street right after the 1917 fire. Her son Eustace stands beside her and behind them one can see the rubble left by the fire. (Courtesy Herndon Historical Society, J. Berkley Green Collection.)

The bridge pictured here was the Sugarland Run Bridge and was built in the manner of many at this time. It provided a route from the Herndon area to Dranesville and for many years could still be seen from Route 7. The bridge was south of Route 7, a short distance from the intersection with Dranesville Road. (Courtesy Alice M. Burton.)

This picture—taken before the 1917 fire—was shot from Station Street looking east toward Monroe Street. Buggies on the left wait for the drivers, and on the south side of the street a woman appears to be cleaning windows. At nightfall the gaslights on the right would be lit. (Courtesy Alice M. Burton.)

This is a photograph taken in the 1990s of the Green Funeral Home. Today known as Adams-Green Funeral Home, it had its beginning in 1885. Thomas E. Reed established the business, which later his son Thomas E. Reed II owned and operated. In 1954, J. Berkley Green purchased the business and property. After Berkley Green's death Chris and Kathryn Adams purchased it.

Standing by the railroad tracks and looking north, one would see a number of buildings, and each housed a business. They were Chamblin's Pharmacy, the bank, a shoe shop, a barbershop, the A&P grocery store, and Duddings Hardware. The A&P building was at the intersection of Station and Pine Streets. (Courtesy Herndon Historical Society, J. Berkley Green Collection.)

Wilkin's store was located at the southwest corner of the Elden and Spring Street intersection. Pictured here are Clarence "Nap" Lee, Elizabeth Groseclose Dunn, and Mr. M.T. Wilkins. Today Jimmy's Tavern is located in this building. (Courtesy Herndon Historical Society, J. Berkley Green Collection.)

In this photograph you are looking west on Elden Street. The large building on the right was a mill lost in the 1937 fire. The fire also destroyed the home by the mill. (Courtesy Herndon Historical Society, J. Berkley Green Collection.)

In the early 1900s this building was Claude G. Stephenson's Real Estate building and also provided space for the Herndon Post Office. Later, it was acquired by the Nachman family and was a clothing store. The building is on Lynn Street in the town-center area. (Courtesy Herndon Historical Society, J. Berkley Green Collection.)

Here one is looking north on Monroe Street from the intersection of Pine and Monroe Streets. The street ran out to the area known as Cooktown, so named after the former owner of the property (a Mr. Cook). The fence for the Congregational church is on the left. The house seen on the left was replaced with an office building. (Courtesy Alice M. Burton.)

This house, known as the Yellow House, was the home of Mr. and Mrs. Thomas Reed before 1900. The building was originally located where the funeral home is today. For a short time it served as a school. (Courtesy Herndon Historical Society, J. Berkley Green Collection.)

Dr. E.L. Detwiler had this house for his medical office. The building is located on Pine Street across from the former location of the Congregational church. Dr. Detwiler's home was on Third Street. (Courtesy Herndon Historical Society, J. Berkley Green Collection.)

E.L. Robey had a drugstore at the corner of Station and Pine Streets, where the Walker building had been located. Through the years the building has had several uses, including Rhor's Five and Dime Store, the Tortilla Factory, and today Zeffirelli's. (Courtesy Herndon Historical Society, J. Berkley Green Collection.)

This photograph, taken looking west on Pine Street, shows some of the buildings along the street. Businesses are, from left to right, Robey's Drug Store and house, Oliver's Shoe Shop and house, and the Sterns' house. (Courtesy Alice M. Burton.)

Members of Herndon's band, dressed in uniform, are pictured in the town-center area with the train and depot in the background. This may have been the day of a War Rally. (Courtesy Herndon Historical Society, J. Berkley Green Collection.)

Seen here is the interior of Mr. Ben McGuire's grocery store. The store was located on the southeast corner of the intersection of Elden and Spring Streets. The building was taken down in the 1950s and replaced with the present brick structure at the site.

This telephone switchboard was located on Pine Street. Alice White (left) and Sylvia Wenzel Bridges (right) are taking care of incoming and outgoing calls. At this time, if the fire siren went off one could call the switchboard and inquire as to where the fire was located. (Courtesy Herndon Historical Society, J. Berkley Green Collection.)

After the 1917 fire an official fire department was organized, and R.S. Crippen was appointed fire chief. In 1950, a new two-story station was constructed on Spring Street. Due to a shortage of space at the elementary school in the 1950s, the second story was used for classrooms for a period of time. (Courtesy Herndon Historical Society, J. Berkley Green Collection.)

The Town Hall was constructed in 1938 as a WPA project funded by the government. The Herndon Post Office was on the first floor with the entrance on the east side. On the second floor there was space for town offices, while the basement provided a meeting room and a temporary lock-up room.

This aerial view, taken in the 1970s, shows the business section of Herndon. The 1938 town hall and the train depot are within the triangle on the lower left side. Citizens National Bank with the addition (with dormers) is in the center of the photograph. Duddings and the long building behind it are across the street from the bank. Some of Herndon's early apartments and townhouses are in the upper right area.

Two

FARMERS, MERCHANTS, AND OTHERS

Ben Middleton and his family are standing in front of the barn at Horsepen Farm in the Floris community. Ben Middleton came to the Herndon area from Yorkshire, England, at the age of seven with his father and brother Brook, age fourteen. From their arrival in 1872 until 1987, Middleton family members owned and operated Horsepen Farm.

It was the summer of 1977 when this photograph was taken at the McNair farm at Floris. The field of barley had been cut and Bob McNair was checking the grain, which had been loaded into the wagon bed.

The Beeker Lowe family came to Chantilly from Low Gap, North Carolina, in 1935. The farm Mr. Lowe purchased had been used as a "way station" for distributing products from an evergreen factory located in Low Gap to places such as Clarendon in Arlington. Mr. Lowe built a barn, dairy house, and silos on the property, then joined the other dairy farmers in the area and shipped milk to the Washington market.

William Harmon Kephart, who lived in Herndon, began weaving carpets when he was only 15 years old. Mr. Kephart was following in his father's footsteps and even used the same loom. He first worked at the Rock Bridge Woolen Mills near Lincoln, which his father had built. In addition to making rugs, Mr. Kephart also made several types of chairs in his shop.

This is a photograph of the farm buildings at Leeton (west of Sully Plantation), the home of the W.W. Wagstaff family. From left to right are an icehouse, carriage house, stable, bank barn, corncrib, and machinery shed. One could go from Route 50, onto the Leeton farm road, by Sully then to Centreville Road. Due to the farm gates not many took this route.

Ernest Scasser lived in the Floris community just off West Ox Road on Pinecrest Road. In addition to farming his own acres, Ernest worked for other farmers when needed and often provided a team of horses. After his sister died and the original two-story home burned, Scasser constructed a cabin for himself.

Manly Hutchison operated this sawmill and a gristmill at Floris. The mill was powered by water from Frying Pan Branch, which ran through the southeast corner of his property. The mill was destroyed by fire. The Floris United Methodist Church is building a new church on this site.

This photograph shows W.O Harrison's General Merchandise Store, which was located just east of the Route 7–Dranesville Road intersection. To the right of the store can be seen a corner of the Harrison home. Today David Harrison, following in his father's footsteps, runs Dranesville Auto Service at this location.

Jenkins General Merchandise was located on Route 7 across the lane from the Dranesville tavern. The store and tavern were run by members of the Jenkins family. The store disappeared many years ago and the tavern was moved from its original location when Route 7 was widened.

Edgar E. Gillette built a number of houses in Herndon before 1950. Among those constructed were his own home at 760 Grace Street, Russell Gillette's home at 869 Vine Street, Wynkoop home at 811 Elden, Mahoney home at 836 Elden, McGuire home at 840 Elden, Hanes home at 873 Vine, Kidwell home at Elden and Ferndale, and the Hutchison home at 1000 Monroe.

W. Floyd Middleton was another property owner and businessman in Herndon. One business he had was a store named the Herndon Emporium, and he was also involved in real estate.

Crop farming was the main land use of the Cockerill farm at Floris. However, they also ran a business that included custom hauling and sales of building products and machinery. This photograph shows the unloading of a gasoline tank for Bloomer and Dave Horn at their Herndon garage in the 1930s. It looks questionable, but it worked!

Sunset Hills Farm was not only a large dairy farm in western Fairfax County, but also the home of "Virginia Gentleman" and "Fairfax County" bourbon whiskey. This is an aerial view of a portion of the 7,000 acres, or 11 square miles, which Mr. A. Smith Bowman purchased in 1927. In 1961, nearly all of the property was purchased by Robert Simon for the community of Reston.

William (Dutch) Middleton and his son Ben stand with two of their dairy animals. The Middleton family had a herd of registered Holstein cows and shipped to the Washington market. In the summer the Middletons often took animals to shows and fairs.

This is an aerial view of the Clyde Patton farm, which was located at the intersection of Centreville and McLearen (Shear) Roads in the Floris community. The Pattons came to Fairfax County from West Virginia in the early 1900s.

H. Arnold Greear was a rural mail carrier from the Herndon Post Office for 29 years. He delivered mail from Herndon out Monroe Street to the Floris community and beyond. He is pictured beside the official postal mail wagon *c.* 1926.

O.C. "Huck" Downs and his Chantilly Mercantile Store were fixtures in the Chantilly neighborhood. Behind him is Route 50, a paved two-lane road. Mr. Sid Wrenn started the store in 1904, he sold it to R.C. Morris in 1927, and Morris sold to Downs in 1941. Haywood Lowe purchased the business in 1964, and he sold to Buddy Barnett in 1978. The store burned in 1981, and Barnett relocated further west on Route 50.

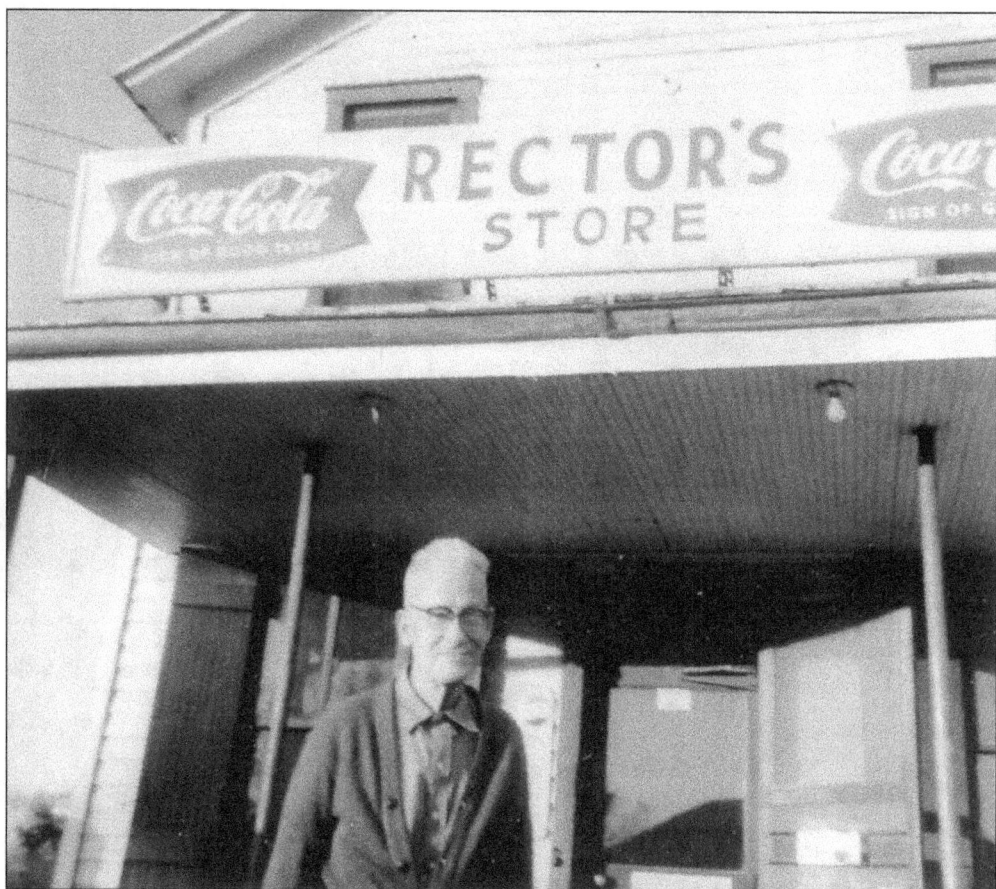

Russell E. Rector stands in front of his store, which was located on Route 50 in the Pleasant Valley community. Sold here were basic grocery items used by families in the neighborhood and by passing motorists. In addition to shopping at his store, area residents went to Herndon and Fairfax to shop. Across from Mr. Rector's store was a garage owned and operated by Benton Hutchison.

Bowman's Store at Floris was a place to pick up a loaf of bread or other items, get some gasoline, have a coke, or visit with the Bowmans. Eventually the Bowmans added new and used furniture to items for sale. Arliss Bowman purchased the store from Mrs. Annie Walker in 1932.

Here is a photograph showing the intersection of Route 50 and Centreville Road at Chantilly. The large brick building was owned by Frank Dunn and had a garage on the ground floor and an apartment on the second floor. After Mr. Dunn closed the garage this area was rented out.

This garage was located on Elden Street in Herndon. Shown in this photograph are automobiles of the day, workmen, and Mr. Bloomer Horn. Bloomer Horn and his brother Dave were co-owners of the property. Later another building was constructed in front of this one, and it is still in use. Today it is known as Horn Motors.

Walter Farr spent many years as a resident of the town of Herndon and was the third individual elected to the position of fire chief for the Herndon Volunteer Fire Department. He and his wife lived on Spring Street. (Courtesy of Alice M. Burton.)

John Middleton is pictured driving in from the cornfield at Horsepen Farm with a wagonload of corn. With new modern machinery it does not take as long to harvest crops—but we now have no crops!

After serving as Herndon's police force for a number of years, Vernon Cockerille retired in early 1950. He never owned or drove an automobile; instead he depended upon the next passing motorist to give him a ride to follow a violator. He and his wife lived at the corner of Nash and Spring Streets. (Courtesy Herndon Historical Society, J. Berkley Green Collection.)

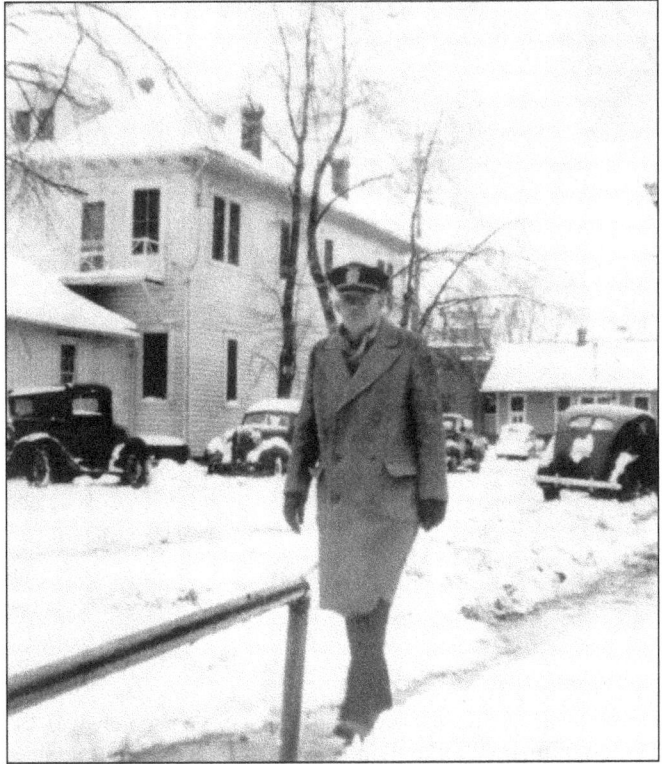

Tony's Barber Shop was located on Station Street close to the bank. The shop was first operated by Irving Wheeler, and later by Tony Brocato.

Pictured here is Rohr's Five and Dime Store, which was located at the corner of Pine and Station Streets. This building was constructed on the site of the former Walker building, and the business was owned by the Rohr family of Manassas. Next door was a building that housed several different restaurants. The roof shown behind this building is that of St. Joseph's Catholic Church.

Porter Hutchison, of Chantilly, lends a hand in the kitchen area at Costello's in Chantilly. The shop was next door to Smith's Farm Machinery and was a good place to stop for a morning cup of coffee.

This is a photograph of the Chantilly Fire House located at the intersection of Walney Road and Route 50. The land for the building was a part of the J. Bryant Smith farm and was donated to the fire department by Mr. Smith. Today, a new station is across the road on Vernon Street. (Courtesy Fairfax County Library Photographic Archive.)

Shown here is a "bumper" crop of wheat being harvested at Bloomfield Farm at Dranesville. It was 1930, and the county agent came to see the outstanding crop Mr. Frank Hammond had grown. The house at Bloomfield was built in 1858 with brick made on the property.

Joseph Fleming of Pleasant Valley is pictured chopping wood for the home fires. Mr. Fleming returned to his farm after serving as a private in Company A, 6th Regiment Virginia Cavalry, Confederate States Army. He enlisted on September 25, 1862, at Paris, Virginia.

VOTE FOR

BERNARD G. BROWN

Democratic Candidate for Congress

Repeal 18th Amendment
Do Not Cancel European Debts
Keep Home Markets for Home Farmers
Keep Home Jobs for Home Men

VOTE FOR the candidate who is 100% for the National Platform and Candidate

Bernard Brown was counted among those who owned a farm within the town limits. In addition to farming Mr. Brown was interested in politics, and in 1932, he ran as the Democratic candidate for Congress from the Eighth District against Howard W. Smith. Others who owned and operated dairy farms within the town included John and Freeland Young; Bentley Harrison; Isaiah, George and Harry Bready; Dr. Bernard Poole; and Harry Bicksler.

48

Richard Thoesen, mayor of Herndon, is shown presenting an award of appreciation to H. Ben Peck in 1987. Ben Peck was retiring as superintendent of public works.

Bank directors for Herndon Central Fidelity Bank pose for their annual photograph. All are residents of the town of Herndon or the outlying area. The directors are, from left to right, (front row) Thom Hanes and John Middleton; (back row) O.C. Downs, Lewis Bradley, William Hoofnagle, Holden Harrison, B.E. Werner, Melvin Nachman, and John McDaniel.

These advertisements appeared in a newspaper directory published in Fairfax County in 1930.

Three

FAMILIES, FRIENDS, AND HOMES

Mr. and Mrs. Graham James Jr. (Mary Anna Gillette) are pictured with their daughter Mary Ann. The James family moved from the farm in the Chantilly/Pleasant Valley area to Herndon in 1952. Graham established a home-building business and became an active member of the community. He served as mayor of Herndon from 1957 to 1960.

Mr. and Mrs. Dallas Hutchison (Ethel Nickell) of Chantilly are enjoying a break in their day's work as they sit on the porch of their farm home. An Adirondack chair, a type found on many porches and in yards during the 1930s and later, provides seating for the Hutchisons.

Russell Edward Rector and Irene Beulah Shirley were married on February 2, 1923, in Baltimore, Maryland. The family lived in the Pleasant Valley community where Mr. Rector operated a store, and the Rector home served as a voting precinct for many years.

Burton family members are pictured in July 1933 at the family home on Monroe Street. The home was later demolished when Monroe Street was widened. Standing from left to right are Bert, Charles, Willis, Amy, Harry, and George. Their father, Charles Burton, is seated in front of them.

Chantilly was the home location for the Beeker Lowe family while farming and later. Mr. Lowe moved from farming to construction and development and developed the Ox Hill subdivision. Pictured here are, from left to right, (front row) Edwin; (middle row) Irene and Louise; (back row) Dale, Beeker, and Haywood.

Pleasant Valley residents Walter and Lutie Presgrave are shown with their grandson Russell Presgrave. They are pictured in the yard of their home, which was located on Route 50.

Mrs. Virginia (McFarland) Greear, who lived with her Uncle Fleming, grew up in the Floris community. In the 1940s, Virginia and Arnold Greear of Herndon married and moved to the Greear family home. Due to her deep interest in the area, Virginia acquired the title of town historian and found delight in sharing her knowledge with others. (Courtesy Alice M. Burton.)

Alice Mae Burton lived with her parents, George and Lena Burton, on Wood Street in Herndon. Alice Mae's grandfather was G.C. Burton, stationer and news-dealer in Herndon. Photographs he had used to make postcards sold in his shop are used in this book. Many photographs in the Green collection were also from his shop. (Courtesy Alice M. Burton.)

Mrs. Arthur Wynkoop (Virgie) is pictured at 100 years old. For many years Mrs. Wynkoop ran a beauty shop in her home on Elden Street, and she later rented rooms to workers in the area. She was an active member of St. Timothy's Episcopal Church, and at the age of 100 she wrote an interesting history of the town of Herndon.

Mr. and Mrs. Townsend Harrison (Dorothy Ambler) sold their farm acreage on Centreville Road and built a new home on McLearen Road. Before long their lovely home and pond were taken for Dulles Airport. Their next move was to Front Royal; however, not many years went by before Route 66 took a part of this property. Progress moves in various ways.

Dressed and ready for Sunday school, three Cockerill children wait for others to join them. Pictured are, from left to right, (front row) Margaret and Jim; (back row) Katherine. The picture was taken in 1935, and they are seated on the porch steps of their home in Floris.

Virginia Heglar Clarity is pictured here as a young child wearing a dress her mother crocheted for her. She has always called Herndon home, has remained interested in its history, and gives time as a volunteer to projects within the town. Stop by and see her dress at the museum.

Mr. and Mrs. Barbour Hutchison (Mary Aud) and their family lived on Monroe Street for many years. Later their daughters Jane and Audrey built homes on the same street. Pictured here are Jane and her husband Glen Hawthorn working in their yard.

When speaking of early educators in the Herndon/Floris area, Elizabeth and Emma Ellmore's names always come to mind. The two of them spent their working years in the field of education and each taught at Floris and Herndon. Elizabeth and Emma grew up in the Floris community; however, both spent their retirement years in Herndon.

Mr. and Mrs. Arliss Bowman lived in the Floris community from 1932 until the late 1950s. After renting the community store, which Mr. Bowman's father had run, they purchased the property from Mrs. Annie Walker. After their son Robert returned from service in 1955, they moved to Loudoun County and he ran the business.

The Moffett children shown here, five sisters and a brother, grew up in Herndon in a home on Van Buren Street. The family is, from left to right, (front row) Beverly and Virginia; (middle row) Elma, Mary Ellen, and Betty; (back row) Bill. Elma Moffett Mankin had the position of secretary for both the earlier high school-elementary school complex and the new Herndon Elementary School on Dranesville Road.

Berkley Green was a family member in a way special to all. He saw families through sad times and could always lift our spirits. Berkley will also be remembered for his generosity toward community projects.

Sisters Edith, Ruth, and Betty McGuire are pictured in front of their family home in Herndon. The young women grew up in the McGuire home on Elden Street. Their father, Ben McGuire, had a grocery store on the southeast corner of Elden and Spring Streets.

The children of Mr. and Mrs. Robert Merchant (Dolly McFarland) are pictured in from of their grandmother Ruth Shillingburg's home in Floris. In the front row is Debbie, and in the back row are Diane, Ronnie, and Keith. It is Easter and they have their baskets ready for an egg hunt and fun.

The Curtis McFarlands (Ruth Simms) were photographed about 1936 in the yard of their home on West Ox Road in the Floris community. Curtis had a shoe repair shop in Herndon. People always looked forward to the colorful and lovely flowers Ruth grew in the summer. Ruth celebrated her 101st birthday in May 2004. In the front row are Lou Ella and Dolly; in the back row are Curtis and Ruth.

Mr. and Mrs. Harry Middleton (Eunice Milam) celebrated their 50th wedding anniversary with a reception at the Floris United Methodist Church. The Middletons were married in her home church in Danville, Virginia on June 27, 1925. Mrs. Middleton was a member of the Herndon Baptist Church and Mr. Middleton a member of the Floris church.

Mr. and Mrs. William Middleton (Sarah Patton) pose with their children Ben and Janie. They are seated on the steps of the Patton home, which was located at the intersection of McLearen (Shear) and Centreville Roads. The Patton family moved to the Floris community from West Virginia in the early 1900s.

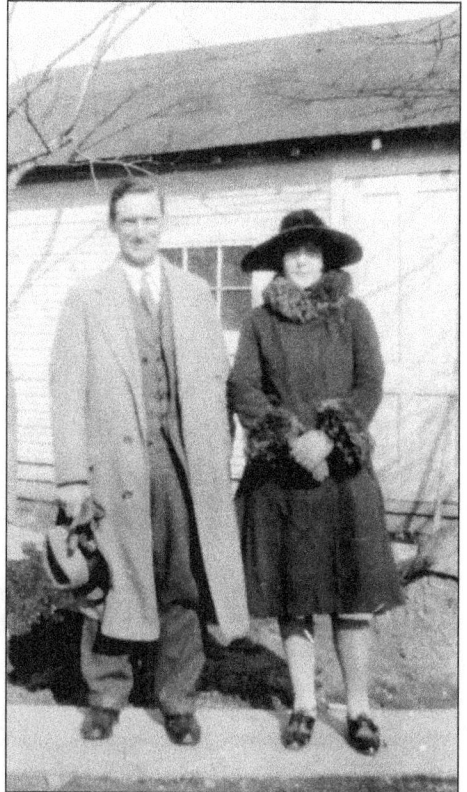

Alice Hutchison of Pleasant Valley and Irvin Harrison of Floris are pictured on their wedding day, December 31, 1926. The couple were married in Washington, D.C., and settled in the Floris community.

Winnie Lee (Brown) Hutchison Higgins and her sister Barbara (Brown) Gratto are shown playing with their Christmas dolls. The Browns moved to Floris when their father, Lee, went into service for World War II.

Mr. and Mrs. Will Middleton (Mary Bradley) of Floris celebrated their 50th wedding anniversary with a party for family and friends at their farm home on West Ox Road. The Middletons were both members of the Floris Methodist Church and were the first couple to be married in the new church. The church was completed in 1896, and they were married in 1897.

Friends and relatives pose for a special photograph at the Robert Harrison home place on Centreville Road. Seen here are, from left to right, Austin Wagstaff, Holden Harrison, Hope Fleming, Irvin Harrison, and Ray Harrison.

Katharine Harrison and Hallie Nickell grew up on neighboring farms in the Floris community and both taught school. In the summer of 1925, they attended the University of Virginia and were members of a study group—along with Sadie Detwiler of Herndon and Fannie Johnson of Clifton—that compiled a geography supplement for Fairfax County.

Pictured here are Middleton relatives who lived in different communities in the area. They are spending a summer afternoon together at the home of Mr. and Mrs. Lacey Nalls (Polly Middleton) in Chantilly.

Dressed up and posing for the photographer are Hilda, John, Mary, and Ben Peck. Mr. and Mrs. Frank Peck (Helen Middleton) of Floris are parents to the children.

Anna Lou (Steele) Bradley is shown in the yard of her parents Mr. and Mrs. A.E. Steele's home in Herndon with her children Ben and Bonnie. Anna Lou, husband Lewis Bradley, and children Ben, Bonnie, Sandra, and Allen lived in the Floris community.

Edna Landis Middleton lived on the family farm with her brother John and his family. Known to family and friends as "Sis," she stayed busy with work she enjoyed, including growing flowers and vegetables in a large garden and quilting in the winter months. "Sis" also enjoyed sharing the results of her work.

This was the original two-part log house constructed by the Cockerill family in the middle 1700s in the community of Floris. After building and moving into a home on the north side of West Ox Road, two other new families made use of this log house. Still later members of the Cockerill family built a home at the corner of Monroe Street and West Ox Road.

This Hutchison house is located in Pleasant Valley on a portion of the over-1,000-acre grant made to Andrew Hutchison in 1726. Early use of the land is not recorded, but like others in the area it eventually became a dairy farm. The first documentation of a dwelling on the property is found in the 1790 census. Today it is a part of the Lafayette Business Center.

Conrad Shear, son of Stephen Shear, is shown walking across the south lawn at Sully Plantation. The Shear family owned Sully from 1874 to 1911 as the property passed from father to son. The last of the large boxwoods shown here was lost in 2004.

The home called Elden was built by John Coleman in 1794. Mr. Coleman owned over 300 acres and his property was referred to as Elden Fruit Farm. This house was home to a number of families through the years; however, this photograph shows members of the Bowers family. A family cemetery, also a part of the property, was saved when the property was sold for development. (Courtesy Herndon Historical Society, J. Berkley Green Collection.)

Leeton, the home of the W.W. Wagstaff family, was west of Sully Plantation. This photograph taken about 1910 shows the house as it was when the Wagstaff family moved to the Chantilly area. The side porch on the right was later enclosed to make an office for Mr. Wagstaff, and the following owners removed the front porch. Leeton, the house, farm buildings, and land, were taken for Dulles International Airport in 1958. (The Turberville home on Walney Road, in Chantilly, also carries the name Leeton.)

Dr. Ben Detwiler, the dentist, had this Elden Street house built in 1890 to serve as his home and office. Herndon resident Charles Reed was the builder. Later, a separate building was constructed for the dental office. Four generations of Detwilers enjoyed this home; however, in time it became too large for one individual and Dr. Detwiler's granddaughter Roberta Keys sold the property. (Courtesy Herndon Historical Society, J. Berkley Green Collection.)

Early members of the Cross family were in the Chantilly-Centreville area by the middle 1700s. The original house, constructed by Benjamin Cross, burned in 1905 while the present one, pictured here, was built in 1907 on the same foundation. Although the surrounding land has been developed, the 1907 house remains.

This farmhouse was built on land Elijah White gave to his daughter Ada and her husband Isaac Long. The house dates to the late 1800s and was located on West Ox Road just east of Horsepen Run. Both general and dairy farming were done here through the years. The house and other buildings were taken down and replaced by a housing development in the 1980s.

This house was home to Bertie Poston when she lived in Sunset Hills. Miss Poston was well known in the area for her artistic ability, and an example of her work is in the Bowman House today. Many who were patients of Dr. Ernest Shull remember the fine portrait she painted of him. (Courtesy Herndon Historical Society, J. Berkley Green Collection.)

Cornelia Lee Turberville and Charles Calvin Stuart built a home on the northern half of land her great-grandfather George Tuberville had patented in 1727. She then named the home Chantilly after her grandfather's plantation on the Northern Neck. The house the Stuarts built was lost in a fire but was replaced by the large home shown here. When a post office was established in the area in 1830, it too carried the name Chantilly. The new house and buildings carried the name Chantilly Farms and the last owners, Mr. and Mrs. William Lohman, operated a dairy farm. (Courtesy Herndon Historical Society, J. Berkley Green Collection.)

J.J. Darlington owned a large property in Herndon located south of Washington (Elden) Street and east of Monroe Street. The large and rather fancy home there when he purchased the property had been built by A.J. Downing. Mr. Darlington gave land for the Herndon Baptist Church to be built on and stone for the church came from his quarry. When he held his annual Labor Day lawn party, town residents were included. In time the house was turned into apartments and then taken down in the 1950s. (Courtesy Herndon Historical Society, J. Berkley Green Collection.)

The Russell Rector family of Pleasant Valley lived in this home, which was located on Route 50 next to their store. Constructed in the late 1800s or early 1900s, it shows the traditional design and style of the time. The majority of the country homes in this area were painted white with the house trim painted white, dark green, or black. In the summer many homes had canvas awnings placed at the windows and on porches. This photograph of the Rector children seated on the porch steps was taken in 1933.

Mr. and Mrs. A.E. Steele (Annie) owned this home located on Nash Street. The Steeles and their daughters Kathryn and Anna Lou were active in the Herndon Baptist Church and in their community. Anna Lou (Steele) Bradley taught at Floris Elementary School for many years.

Joseph and Lucinda Fleming and their children lived in this house at Pleasant Valley in the late 1800s. Later, it was the home of their daughter Araminta and her husband, Philip Alexander Hutchison.

The large square building at the intersection of Third and Grant Streets was Dr. Ed Detwiler's home. His office was located on Pine Street across from the Congregational church. Dr. Ed and Dr. Ben Detwiler, the first in Herndon to own automobiles, caused much excitement when they drove through town. (Courtesy Herndon Historical Society, J. Berkley Green Collection.)

Pictured here is the Floris home of Mr. and Mrs. Wilson McNair (Virginia Nickell) and their children Louise and Robert. The McNairs operated a successful dairy business and like other farmers shipped their milk to the Washington market. The McNairs took an active role in church, school, and community projects. The home was incorporated into the development of the farm but later taken down.

Mr. and Mrs. Graham James Sr. and family lived in this home on their farm in the Chantilly-Pleasant Valley area. The James sons—Graham Jr. and Roy—worked with their father running a large dairy-farm operation. The former farmland is now part of a Fairfax County Park Authority park.

The Heitmuller home, built about 1900, was located on Herndon's Spring Street east of Van Buren until the late 1980s. At that time, it was one of two houses Steve Mitchell moved to Nash Street. The other house was the Patton home, which had been on Van Buren Street. Both houses were moved, redone, and resold.

Pictured here is the Floris home of Mr. and Mrs. Ray Harrison (Virginia), which was constructed about 1936. In the background of the photograph one can see the farm buildings for Dairy Lou Farm. Ray Harrison and his brother Holden Harrison farmed together at Dairy Lou for a number of years.

This is a photograph of the George C. Burton home located at Spring and Wood Streets. The building, which is similar to a Sears Roebuck house plan, was constructed by Mr. Burton in 1920. This was the second house he built on Wood Street.

Located on Park Street in Herndon, this home belonged to Asbury Harrison. Mr. Harrison was one of the individuals who owned and operated a dairy farm in the town of Herndon, and in addition to the Herndon farm he also had a farm in the Floris community.

This was the home of Mr. and Mrs. Walter Presgrave (Lutie) and their children Gilbert, Carroll, Edwin, Stanley, and Virginia. The home is located on Route 50 in the Pleasant Valley community and is one of the few earlier homes still standing.

Mr. and Mrs. Allen Bradley (Mate) lived in the Floris community with their sons Lewis and Austin. The Bradley farm was on West Ox Road just west of today's Fairfax County Parkway. Like a number of others the Bradleys had a dairy operation and shipped milk to the Washington market. The farm was sold for development and family members moved to Florida.

Four

CHURCHES
AND SCHOOLS

This photograph is of Frying Pan Springs Meeting House, which is located on Centreville Road in the community of Floris. Early stories state the building was constructed in 1727, or the present structure was built over an earlier one, or it was originally a tobacco barn. Records show the members requested permission to build a meeting house in 1783, were meeting in 1791, and continued until 1968.

Oak Grove Baptist Church, which is located off Sterling Road or Route 606, was started in 1868. In 1958 their church was lost by fire, but the group rebuilt and continued. In 2002 a new church was constructed for the busy and growing congregation. (Courtesy Herndon Historical Society, J. Berkley Green Collection.)

Mount Pleasant Baptist Church had its beginning on Coppermine Road in the Floris community after 1850 and has continued through the years in a pattern of growth. In 1982 they moved to a new building across the road, then in 1999 another step was taken to a larger and very beautiful church on Squirrel Hill.

The first church in Herndon was the Northern Methodist Episcopal Church, which was built in 1872 at the corner of Elden and Center Streets. Today another denomination uses this building. (Courtesy Herndon Historical Society, J. Berkley Green Collection.)

By 1915 a group desiring a Southern Methodist Church in Herndon built a church on Spring Street. Later, in 1938, the two groups joined as one and continued at this location. Although they added on in the 1960s, church growth directed they build again. In 1987, a new Methodist church was built on Bennett Street. (Courtesy Alice M. Burton.)

The congregation for St. Joseph's Catholic Church had their first building constructed in 1925 on Pine Street. Years later, in the 1960s as the area's population increased a new complex was built on Peach Street. Today, they are completing construction for an enlarged school and other related buildings. (Courtesy Herndon Historical Society, J. Berkley Green Collection.)

The Congregational Church was built in 1873 at the corner of Monroe and Pine Streets. In time the Herndon Presbyterian Church members joined this group. In 1959, the Floris Presbyterian Church members became a third party and a new name was chosen—Trinity Presbyterian Church. Today, an office building replaces the original building and the present church is located on Dranesville Road. (Courtesy Alice M. Burton.)

There has been a Methodist church at Pleasant Valley since 1894. Today, though many early families have moved on, several of them are still represented. An active congregation continues here, and in recent years a mirror image of the 1894 building was constructed.

Chantilly Baptist Church is located just west of the Centreville Road and Route 50 intersection at Chantilly. Recently this congregation completed a rebuilding project. The finished building is very beautiful and provides for the needs of their growing congregation.

St. Timothy's Episcopal Church started as a Mission church; however, by 1871 they had relocated to Grace and Vine Street to a building that had been a factory. A new church had been built by 1880 at Grace and Elden Streets, and then 80 years later they made another move, this time to Van Buren/Spring Street. The structure on Grace was purchased by the Masons for their organization. (Courtesy Herndon Historical Society, J. Berkley Green Collection.)

The Herndon Baptist Church located at the intersection of Monroe and Elden Streets was built in 1900. J.J. Darlington gave the land for the building and the stone came from his quarry. The windows and doorframes were made by William Harmon Kephart and the lumber was donated by Weston Kephart. (Courtesy Herndon Historical Society, J. Berkley Green Collection.)

84

This is a postcard of the original parsonage for the Herndon Baptist Church. When the church members built a new parsonage for their minister on Van Buren Street, this became a home for the Harding family. Today, it is known to Herndon residents as Harding Hall. (Courtesy Alice M. Burton.)

This is the parsonage that was home for ministers who served churches on the Pleasant Valley Charge. The churches on the charge were not always the same; however, Floris Church was a member in the 1940s. Rev. and Mrs. Woodrow W. Hazlett were the first to live in the new home and are pictured in front of the house. Today Pleasant Valley has a new parsonage at South Riding.

Members of the Ray and Virginia Harrison family are photographed in front of the Methodist church at Pleasant Valley. Above the door is the window the Harrison children gave in honor of their parents. Pictured are, from left to right, Ray and Virginia Harrison, William Harrison, Douglas Harrison, Kim (Mrs. Steve) Harrison, and Polly (Mrs. William) Harrison.

Hutchison siblings are shown at the D.A.R. program held to place a marker at Frying Pan Springs Meeting House in 1993. At this special service a wreath of flowers was placed to honor early members of this church group. Pictured are, from left to right, Wilmer, Bina Ruth Follin, and Lewis and Porter Hutchison.

Before 1955 children of the Floris community often attended Bible school at the Floris Elementary School. At times the Presbyterian and Methodist churches joined together for the summer classes and all children in the area were invited to attend. Pictured here are attendees of one of the young classes.

A group of children at the Pleasant Valley United Methodist Church listen while a Bible story is read to them. Bible school, Sunday school, and children's story time at the Sunday morning service are special times within our Methodist churches.

Members of the Floris United Methodist Church gather for a congregation photograph on their last Sunday at the 1896 building. The first service in the new church was held on Sunday, September 12, 1993. Ten years later the building had been outgrown. Today's plan is to be in another new building by December 2005.

This three-room school, constructed around 1872 and used until 1911, was the second school built in Herndon. The building was remodeled for use as a home in 1912 by A.A. Chamblin. In 1926 it was purchased by Mr. and Mrs. Harry Breckenridge and remained their home until 1970. The next owners were Mr. and Mrs. Donald Levine. (Courtesy Herndon Historical Society, J. Berkley Green Collection.)

Pictured here are the students in the first graduating class at Herndon High School. The photograph was taken in 1897 in front of the school. (Courtesy Herndon Historical Society, J. Berkley Green Collection.)

Students of Herndon Seminary are dressed and ready for a performance. The students are, from left to right, Priscilla Barnes, Elma Middleton, Elma Gillette, Mildred Cooper, Waite Wilkins, Virginia Lang (kneeling), Sophia Crouch (behind Virginia Lang), Margaret Florence, Clara Hutchison, Rosie Voght and Margaret Voght. Mrs. Castleman and her daughters operated the school until 1924. Gen. Robert E. Lee was a cousin to Mrs. Castleman. (Courtesy Herndon Historical Society, J. Berkley Green Collection.)

Miss Ruth Simms (McFarland, Shillingburg) is shown in June 1921 on graduation day following her graduation from Floris Vocational High School. Standing in the family yard she is holding her diploma in one hand and the traditional bouquet of flowers in the other. Ruth later married Curtis McFarland.

This photograph of Herndon High School was taken in 1924. In the 1927–1928 school year the building was lost to fire but was rebuilt. Today Herndon Middle School is on this site on Locust Street. The present high school built in the late 1960s is located off Dranesville Road on Bennett Street. (Courtesy Alice M. Burton.)

This is a photograph of students at Herndon High School. They are pictured in front of the building, which was destroyed by fire. (Courtesy Herndon Historical Society, J. Berkley Green Collection.)

Floris school students stand in front of the schoolhouse built in 1900. This was the second school built on the site; the first was a one room building constructed in 1876. The only students identified are: Mary Cockerill (Lee), front row, third from left; Virginia Mc McFarland (Greear), middle row, second from left; Edna Thompson (Dove), middle row, fifth from left; Welby Cockerill, middle row, far right; and Helen Middleton (Peck), back row, far left.

Students who lived at Sunset Hills attended elementary and high school in Herndon. They caught the W&OD at the Sunset Hills Station and rode it to Herndon in the morning and back in the afternoon. The post office for Sunset Hills was also in the station.

This postcard shows the young women students from the class of 1909 at Floris. The three-room building was constructed in 1900, and in addition to elementary classes, two years of high school were offered.

Students at Floris, both boys and girls, were very active in sports, and since they did not have an indoor court they played on an outdoor one. Pictured here is the girl's basketball team having an afternoon game while parents and community friends watch.

The entire student body of Floris School is pictured here in front of the 1911 school. Elementary grades and two years of high school classes were offered. The principal of the school, Miss Sadie Detwiler, is standing at the end of the second row and is wearing a light skirt and dark jacket. (Courtesy Fairfax County Public Library.)

Students who took part in home economics classes at Floris High School are shown dressed in their uniforms. The classes were held in a privately owned building, which the students named Hominy Hall, located next to the school.

Children at Floris Elementary School are taking part in a spring ritual called the May Pole Dance or Braiding of Ribbons. The teacher is Miss Katie Groh, who was from Herndon but taught at Floris for many years. She was never called anything but "Miss Katie," and all the children loved having her as their teacher. (Courtesy Fairfax County Public Library.)

Pictured here are the Pleasant Valley School and the students attending at the time. Miss Mary Hixon was the teacher and taught all grades. Students from Pleasant Valley would have attended high school at Floris.

Students from Dranesville School are pictured in front of their school. The school—which was located by the present Dranesville Methodist Church—closed in 1931, and the students began attending Herndon Elementary School. In 1964, the building was included as part of an addition to the church. The students would have attended high school in Herndon.

When this photograph was taken, the three-story building at Floris was used for elementary classes, and the four-room building was used as a residence. High school students from the Floris, Chantilly, Pleasant Valley, and Dranesville areas started attending high school in Herndon in 1930. (Courtesy Fairfax County Public Library.)

A new school was built in Herndon for African-American students in the 1950s. The school was located on Sterling Road and provided classes for grades one through seven. A high school for these students, Luther Jackson, was located in Merrifield. In recent years the building has served as office space for Herndon's police force. (Courtesy Fairfax County Public Library.)

At Herndon High School, agriculture was an important subject for many years, even though not all the students who were in the classes lived on farms. Mr. Roy Crabill is pictured here with his students in October of 1940.

After World War II an agriculture class for interested veterans was held at Herndon High School. Joseph Hutchison taught the group and members of the class came from Herndon, Centreville, Chantilly, Floris, Vale, Fairfax, and McLean. Subject matter covered various aspects of farming and related information. Today the farms the men owned, managed, or worked on are filled with houses or commercial buildings.

Pictured here are students in the second grade at Floris Elementary School in 1957. Standing with them is their teacher Nancy Harrison, who grew up in the community, went off to college, and later returned to teach there.

Herndon's homecoming parade each fall has always been a fun time for those attending. Students, parents, business representatives, and friends of students take part in the parade or line the streets to watch while the judges decide the winners. Pictured here are students from Floris Elementary School on the float they created. Mrs. Elizabeth Hanes, the fourth grade teacher, rode with them. These students later attended Herndon High School.

The 1951 Senior Prom for Herndon High School was held in the school auditorium. Decorations were taken care of by the students, music was provided by a small band, and refreshments were seen to by a group of parents.

May Day eventually turned into Health Day at our county schools. With a theme of Greek Sports, Floris students have their picture taken in May 1960. These are members of the rhythm band, and Mark Lowe, third from the left, was the leader.

Mrs. Nina Gibson of Herndon was principal of Floris Elementary School at the 1920 three-story building and moved to the new school in 1955. In addition to being principal, Mrs. Gibson, along with Mrs. Bradley, taught the sixth graders. Mrs. Gibson retired in 1960 and was honored at a reception at the school. Mrs. Betty McNair is presenting Mrs. Gibson with one of her gifts.

Members of the Herndon High School staff pose for an end-of-the-year photograph. The teachers are, from left to right (front row) Katherine White and unidentified; (middle row) ? Williams, unidentified, and Harold Wiler; (back row) Principal Jack Rice, E.J. Heglar, unidentified, and Roy Crabill. This photograph was taken in the early 1930s.

Fairfax County has long been a leader in the field of education and there have been many outstanding individuals to lead the programs. Dudley Page, pictured here, was one of those special teachers and leaders. Dudley graduated from Herndon High School and then returned to teach there. He later became the principal of Herndon Elementary School, giving a total of 30 years to the school system.

Five

LEISURE-TIME ACTIVITIES

Members of a Herndon group enjoy a watermelon feast in August of 1908. They had taken an outing to the Seneca River and enjoyed their picnic on the riverbank. Shown are, from left to right, Miss Lizzie Rucker, George Burton, W. Newhall, Miss Maude Yount, and Miss Ruth Rucker. (Courtesy Alice M. Burton.)

Manly and Nancy Hutchison's grandchildren enjoy a day together at their grandparents home in the Floris community. With a nice lawn to play on and a branch nearby for the older children, a fun day was enjoyed. (Courtesy Alice M. Burton.)

Several Herndon men are on a camping trip and have settled in on the bank of the Seneca River, including, from left to right, Charlie Reed, Claude Yount, and George Burton. (Courtesy Alice M. Burton.)

The group of men pictured here are former members of John S. Mosby's Rangers. The men had gathered for a reunion. (Courtesy Alice M. Burton.)

Mr. and Mrs. Paul Powell of Herndon are shown going out for a carriage ride. Paul Powell enjoyed both riding and working with his horses. He was known to have supplied the horses to pull Santa's sleigh at Christmas and for at least one occasion to have done likewise for the funeral home hearse. (Courtesy Herndon Historical Society, J. Berkley Green Collection.)

Town and area residents turned out for a rally in the town center during World War I. A shipment of flour from the Town of Herndon was being loaded on the train to begin its journey to France. (Courtesy Alice M. Burton.)

Willis H. Burton of Herndon shows off his catch for the day. He and others had been on a fishing outing to Seneca River. The automobile behind him appears to date about 1924. Willis Burton and his brother George often enjoyed a day of fishing.

Seven young women pose in milk bottles, perhaps as the "cream of the farm." They are riding on a float representing Fairfax County and its role in the dairy industry and milk production. The year is 1930, and they are taking part in the Piedmont Dairy Farming Festival parade. (Courtesy Fairfax County Public Library.)

Boys from Miss Grace Beard's summer camp at Rock Hill Farm, near Herndon, are ready to leave for the fair at Floris School. With no truck to use for transportation, they loaded the Guernsey calf into the automobile for the trip of a few miles.

When the Wagstaff family moved to their farm at Chantilly the boys, Eddie and Austin, brought along their Buffalo Springs baseball outfits. Looking for a fun activity, their sisters, Zelma and Helen, decided to suit themselves up in the outfits and pose for a photograph.

Members of the "Over 80 Club" of Herndon pose for a picture session. The occasion was the celebration of George (Uncle George) Harrison's birthday. Octogenarians are, from left to right, (front row) Mrs. John Oliver, 83; Mrs. Victoria Albaugh, 85; Mrs. A.C. Bowers, 82; Mrs. Mildred Wells, 81; and Mrs. James Leith, 90; (back row) Arthur Norbau, 84; E.N. Groff, 86; George Harrison, 81; John Oliver, 83; and Samuel Coleman, 85. (Courtesy Herndon Historical Society, J. Berkley Green Collection.)

James W. Powell is shown on his horse Black Beauty at a Fairfax Hunt Club Meet. James, who lived at Sunset Hills, rode from an early age and was recognized as one of the youngest to ride at the time. He served as "Whip" for the Fairfax Hunt. Mrs. Beverly Coleman is shown giving Black Beauty a treat.

109

A day at the river is enjoyed by young ladies from Pleasant Valley. They are dressed in the latest swimming attire, which includes swimming caps. The women are, from left to right, Virginia Presgrave, Pauline Smith, Lillian Adrian, Kathleen Adrian, and Eleanor Nevitt.

Lee C. Brown of Herndon is seen in a photograph taken about 1934. Not every one had an automobile, but those who had them enjoyed their rides and trips.

Charlie Burton of Herndon (above) and Jack Patton of Floris (below) are pictured ready for trips in their vehicles Not every young man could afford an automobile, and those who could were most proud. The vehicles date from early 1930s.

Family members and visitors at Sunset Hills Farm often enjoyed the inviting landscape at the swimming pool. Flowering shrubs, boxwoods, and evergreens are seen along the path to the home while Adirondack and 1940s chairs beckon one to stop for a spell.

Many of the residents of Herndon and the surrounding area often had the opportunity to visit and picnic at Great Falls. Sunday school picnics and family reunions took place on the park grounds, and riding the merry-go-round was great fun. After severe storms people from the area would drive to the park to view the high water, which was an exciting picture to view.

Children from Floris Elementary School have been taking part in a visit/picnic to the quarry area beyond the school. The classroom teacher for the group was Miss Gladys Thompson. Such an outing at the end of the school year was a special treat.

Members of the Ben Middleton family from Floris are shown on a Sunday outing. The family is, from left to right, grandson John Peck, Hannah Middleton, Ben Middleton, daughter-in-law Elizabeth Buck Middleton holding her son David, and son-in-law, Frank Peck.

This photograph was taken at the old Floris School site on a day the Fairfax County 4-H Fair was being held in the 1950s. On the right is the cook-shack, by the 1911 building is the stage for presentations, and an antique auto is on display. Not shown are the exhibit barn, show ring, and today's equestrian center. The fair continues to be held each August.

It is 1930 and the Floris Home Demonstration Club has been recognized as the "most effective club" in Fairfax County at an area meeting. (Courtesy Fairfax County Public Library.)

These dancers took part in a production called "Floris Follies." The program was presented at Floris Elementary School in the 1930s. Many of the community residents had parts in the program, and Virginia Peck provided the musical score. The performers are, from left to right, Jether Dove, Arliss Bowman, unidentified, Virginia Peck, Principal Bowers, unidentified, and Charlie Austin.

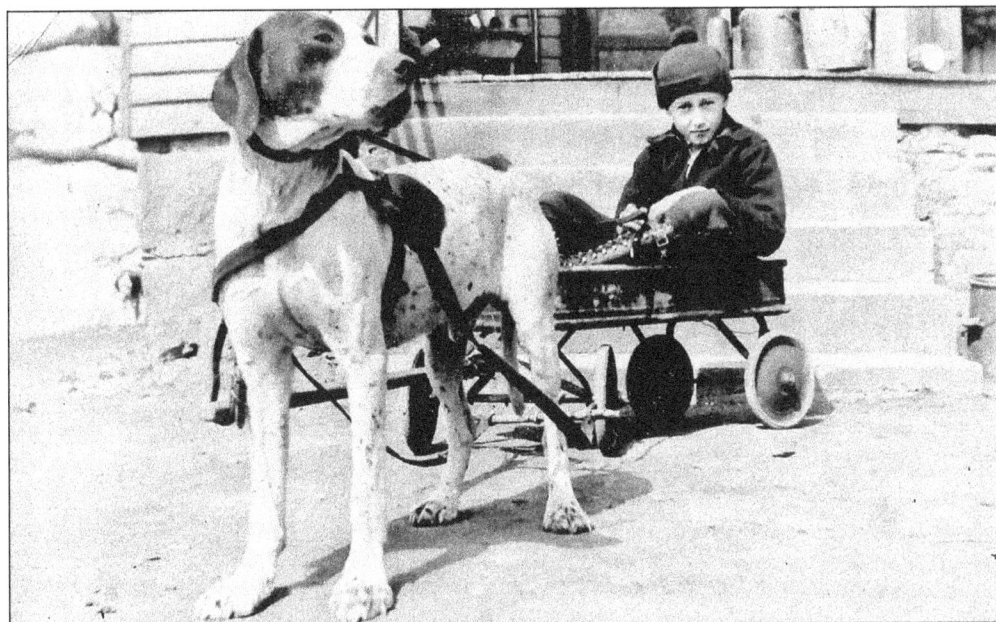

It is March of 1936, and Jim Cross is pictured getting a ride in his wagon while his dog serves as the power. Jim is shown in front of the family home at their farm off Walney Road in Chantilly.

Josephine Evans has her dairy animal washed, brushed, and ready for the 4-H Fair at Floris School. The fair was a fun time, an opportunity to be with friends, and a chance to eat the delightful special food.

In 1980, the torchbearer for the Olympics ran through a section of western Fairfax County. Here he is shown running along Route 50 in the Chantilly community. It was an honor to have our area included in the path taken.

Fairfax County Senior 4-H members are shown attending a social function. Facing the camera, from left to right, are William Harrison, Lewis Leigh, and Dean Gresham; on the side and back, from left to right, are Margaret Fletcher, Pat Patriarca, and Clara Middleton.

Marjorie Gillette and her brother Peck of Herndon ride the merry-go-round at Great Falls Park. The carousel was a special part of any trip to Great Falls, and many churches and organizations went there for their summer picnics. Catching the brass ring was on each rider's mind as they rode their favorite animal.

Members of the Nickell family are gathered at the family homeplace, at Floris, for a summer picnic and celebration of Mr. R.B. Nickell's birthday. Mr. and Mrs. R.B. Nickell moved from West Virginia to Fairfax County in the early 1900s.

Members of the Floris 4-H Club have just listened to a Fire Prevention Week presentation given by W. Herman Kephart. Mr. Kephart was a charter member of the Herndon Volunteer Fire Department and a member of the Fairfax County Fire Commission.

For many years there was an extremely active Herndon Ladies Fire Auxiliary (HVFD) group. They marched in the homecoming parade and sometimes marched in firemen's carnival parades elsewhere. The group was supportive of community projects and purchased the first ambulance for the town. (Courtesy Herndon Historical Society, J. Berkley Green Collection.)

Middleton family members are pictured here at their Horsepen Farm home at Floris. From left to right are (front row) Elizabeth Buck Middleton holding daughter Clara, Ben P. Middleton, Sara Jane Middleton, and David B. Middleton; (back row) Grace Buck, Sadie Detwiler, John Middleton, Edna L. Middleton, and W.D. Buck.

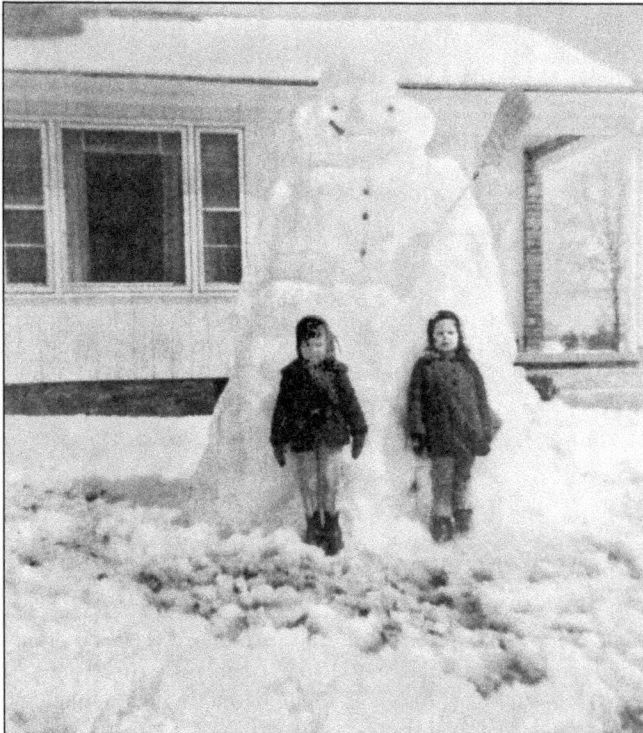

Celeste Lowe and Doris Rollins, best friends and neighbors, decided they needed a bigger-than-life snowman. The girls built the snow sculpture in front of the Lowe home on Lowe Street in Chantilly.

Herndon's Fourth of July picnic has often been held at Bruin Park on Van Buren Street. Hot dogs, sodas, and the usual picnic food is there for all to share, while music and other entertainment is provided for everyone's enjoyment. Hannah Crew, from Floris, is shown dancing to the music of a local group.

Each year on Memorial Day there is a special program at Chestnut Grove Cemetery in Herndon. Individuals from the American Legion and the town lead the program and place memorial wreaths. The cemetery was started in the early 1800s on land that had been purchased by Mrs. Kate Barker. Until 1998, the cemetery was managed by a volunteer board of directors. Today the Town of Herndon owns and operates the cemetery.

Writers for the book *Voices of Chantilly* celebrated publication of their work at a reception at the Chantilly Library in 1996. Twenty-two longtime area residents wrote stories of life in years past in the Chantilly area.

Six

A New Age

An announcement by President Dwight Eisenhower on January 14, 1958, was the first step in changing the face of our area in Fairfax County. The first moving of soil for the building of Dulles Airport took place on September 2, 1958. While the dignitaries watched, this Caterpillar bulldozer pushed the first dirt around.

Ben Burton of Floris is standing beside one of the large—but not the largest—machines brought in to be used at Dulles. C.J. Langenfelder & Sons, Inc. of Baltimore, Maryland, had the prime contract for the work.

H. Ben Peck and son Byron watch as trees are felled and soil moved on the family farm at Floris. Their woods, ponds, and some crop fields were cleared for landing lights and other needed space.

Houses that had been homes along the border of Fairfax and Loudoun Counties were moved across fields and along roads to become new homes in Chantilly and Herndon. Most displaced families found new homes elsewhere.

Construction of the terminal and tower was an interesting process to watch. We ended Sunday afternoon outings by driving by to check it out, and then found it necessary to drive on the runways to check them out.

Once completed the Eero Saarinen–designed building was awesome to view. One found it hard to believe such a change had taken place in this once-quiet area.

The airport received low use in the beginning years and was often referred to as the white elephant in our back yards. However, in time the action started and a surge of people, houses, office space, and automobiles moved in. When steps were taken in 2001 to remember John S. Mosby and his Rangers with a plaque, his rock was there but surrounded by houses.

After Herndon had increased in residents to 20,000+, it became necessary to make some changes. New town offices have been constructed and a larger library has been built. In addition space was set aside for a town green, which provides a place for summer concerts and other activities. In 2002, the Herndon American Legion members placed a memorial on the town green to honor all who have served in military service.

When the most beautiful airplane to fly made its initial appearance at Dulles Airport, we put our work and activities on hold and watched the graceful Concorde come in. In 2003, some of us returned to watch the last flight out. It did not matter if the plane was flying or waiting for take off, it always caught our attention.

www.ingramcontent.com/pod-product-compliance
Lightning Source LLC
Chambersburg PA
CBHW080551110426
42813CB00006B/1277